THE WANTING WAY

 multiverse

Series Editor

Chris Martin

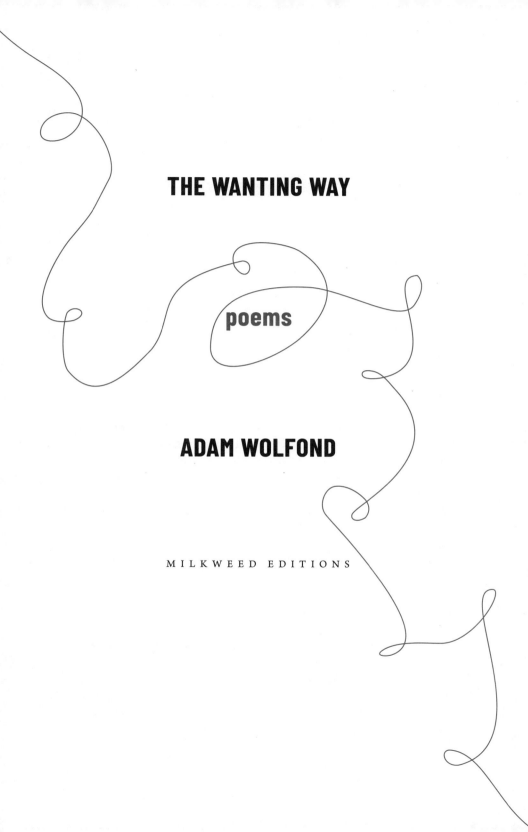

THE WANTING WAY

poems

ADAM WOLFOND

MILKWEED EDITIONS

Published 2022 by Milkweed Editions
Printed in the United States of America
Cover design by Mary Austin Speaker
Cover artwork by Estée Klar
Author photo by Michael Klar
22 23 24 25 26   5 4 3 2 1
First Edition

Library of Congress Cataloging-in-Publication Data

Names: Wolfond, Adam, 2002- author.
Title: The wanting way : poems / Adam Wolfond.
Description: First edition. | Minneapolis, Minnesota : Milkweed Editions,
    2022. | Series: Multiverse | Summary: "The Wanting Way is a confluence
    of diverse ways-rallies, paths, waves, jams, streams, desire lines-that
    converge wherever the dry verbiage of the talking world requires
    hydration"-- Provided by publisher.
Identifiers: LCCN 2022004513 (print) | LCCN 2022004514 (ebook) | ISBN
    9781571315502 (trade paperback) | ISBN 9781571317759 (ebook)
Subjects: LCGFT: Poetry.
Classification: LCC PR9199.4.W64 W36 2022 (print) | LCC PR9199.4.W64
    (ebook) | DDC 811/.6--dc23/eng/20220209
LC record available at https://lccn.loc.gov/2022004513
LC ebook record available at https://lccn.loc.gov/2022004514

Milkweed Editions is committed to ecological stewardship. We strive to align our
book production practices with this principle, and to reduce the impact of our
operations in the environment. We are a member of the Green Press Initiative, a
nonprofit coalition of publishers, manufacturers, and authors working to protect the
world's endangered forests and conserve natural resources. *The Wanting Way* was
printed on acid-free 30% postconsumer-waste paper by Versa Press.

To the world: go toward the way of neurodiversity.

CONTENTS

THE WANTING WAY

The Ways of Yearning

In my mind I am always
thinking
about everything

how to filter it
is the wanting question

It is wanting to follow
the thread

to reach the way
of thoughts

I think the thread
snow
balls

it every chatter
collecting thoughts

and how does one unball
all
we have gathered?

I must follow the thread to the end I ask others to unravel with me

It's not about me
it's us

we
unravel
unball

To reach the end
we must take our beings
and yearn
the moments
together

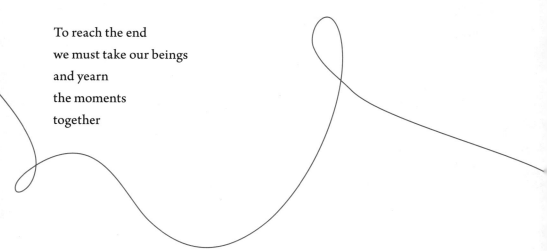

I think a line can move like a map

In Way of Music Water Answers

Like water I am eager
Like water I am thinking
Like water I always move

Like water I am thinking time
open and following eager going
pathways and open going nowhere

I boat on the water the way I want to talk

of the neurodivergent city

I Am the Pace of My Body and Not Language

I think the days of the week
        are paced in the line of rocks
             and the water of the ocean

Water talks by pacing waves against them

Rocks respond by allowing their surfaces to be worn

Time is perceived by the appreciation
      of language but I am
        the (pace) of my body
          and not language

I think there are many times to think about

I want people to understand how hard it is
      to always type

My rhythm is long and continuous
not as noises in my head

The noises are forging want
of the howling wind

The noises are in the want
to talk

But feel the way I always toward the calm body go

4

Time is perceived by the appreciation
of language but I am
the pace of my body
and not language

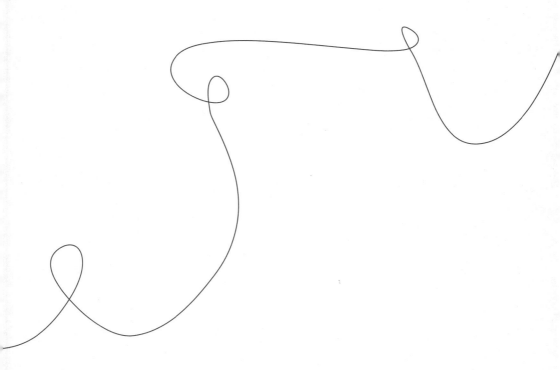

and line the rally that I can feel.

The Language of Lasting

I am like others
but pale is my talking

I am the toast of laughter
because I am always laughing
at people who think I am very stupid

I am person like
a thoughtful passing
of hot water on my tongue

The water sometimes lingers
and too much language
is hot and painful

For others the water is cold
and fast but palm of my hand
is the language of lasting friendship

The hand thinks
with people who support
love and illustrates my language

Lots lingers
in my good body

A Landing Always Answers

Outing the young open (feeling) upward

into the place of work

the walk is when I think the most

and my body is a single pattern

and art is a feeling

inside it

but the way of walking

is also falling

and a landing always answers

so I want to know

why people want me

to always question the ways

I eagerly say what I want

dancing a lot in language

I want places

to answer in the want

of words

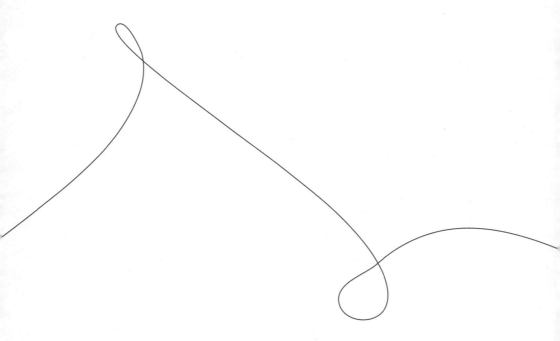

Pacing the way of my poetry to book form

I Plant Watered Words

I laugh at watering words with my typing finger
and I am thinking: water words are really
thinking with thought
I think with   w a t e r
flickering the   l i g h t
                    r a i n   is mastering
thought with landings
that eagerly run and
toward more thoughts
go
a way to write is
to think   water
inside the   b o d y   and
open outside
to the panel of questioning people
about the way I answer
having a thinking body is
the way of watering words

redistribute (*restibule*) to feel the way

A Typology of Water

Rain is mastering thought
with landings that
eagerly run and toward
more thoughts go

Stream of thought
is the pace
of the thinking apparition
of the way thought
is landing

Lake is the pool
of thought
and the always
pleasing calm

Pond the simple pause
of words
opening insides
puttering to more boredom
where the bottom of ponds are still

Ocean is like the inside
of the palpitating heart
where love is pleasing
place of pampering
universe in my head

In my head is my heart

I Am Eating Language All the Time

In the pale morning
language tastes
like really thick foggy air
nasty red words
come to mind

The pale afternoons
are particularly always awful

Good tasting times
are when I am thinking
about water wanting
words to always flow and I
am loving with words

Eager language easy when I am
talking tall orders like wanting toys

I think talking nasty
words really must taste
like great sour candy

I am pleased
when I can say
what's on my mind
I answer like a book
is reading like candy

I think I want to eat(words)all the time

I want real talking and not having
the ability to talk is mostly like good shit

in neurodiverse body.

Algo Rhythm 1

Feel how the real time walk games the space. The gaze is important so go game the space—do it while people are watching and feel the way anxiety is like the long place of time and that is the tool to understand. Then dance the language to describe that feeling. Face the good hard place of language with walking and favorite management knowing that open dance of neurodiverse stimming is feeling the way.

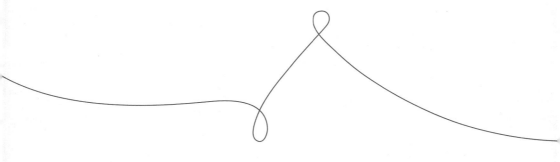

Go to the idea of marginalia

Rushing

The talking
world is like a troubled water
rushing toward my body it feels

Like talking
is always (toward) me
and how

I talk
is the easy way to anger
the easygoing river is

Where talking
feels always true
and noticing ways that

Greedy talks
bother me because
I need

To talk
so careful the dreaming water is easy careful
being yes the feeling questions are water

To my body

To Think Answers Is to Autism Tangled

In a weaving loom
that holds lots of threads
the colors of life
I want to use
and other than
a line

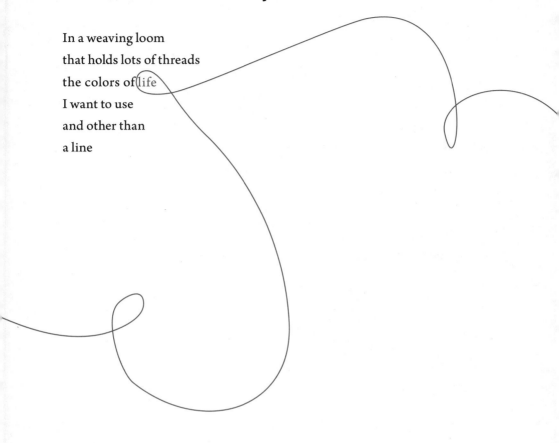

that is paging the ways through

Answers Toward Questions Other Than What Is Autism

Ticcing through the world
is like touching it

The inward rotation of a spiral
is like amazing tall idea
always thinking
around and
out

Inside the world is the question
of easy touch

Good thought moves like fluid water
and the way of water is raining
really into the seething good
cracks of wanting
thought

Mostly I sometimes tic through the world
and that is the way I feel

I feel the world too much so open
bothersome work is to feel
inside pandering
to language

The work is to feel the world
that is touching me

The Maker of Wanting Space

I want to say that I want
to amazing space
think
about the way I move

to think

I (game) the space the way
I open with the body
and the way
I think
which is the way of water

It touches me open and
I am away
with really easy feelings
of dancing for the answering
really rare always rallying
thinking and it is rare with the way
people think

Really way of
touching the world is
the way I am wanting
with my tics

I think that I want the way inside
questions opening the want to
the wanting way which thinks openly

toward the water and I am
thinking about it all
the time

I think that
I want the way inside
questions
opening the want to
the wanting way
which thinks openly
toward the water
and I am
thinking about it
all the time like
eating words

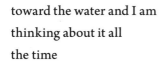

like the ways of the water

Tic and Tap

I tic like a using toy
of tall ideas to tap my way
through the space
of the outside world
and I sometimes game
the space like a backward spiral that
tries to find its way.

I tic because I want to
be settled and I tap
to feel the way the comings arrange
me like a forge
inside my eyes.

I am feeling all
the time
and I am the toy
talker who
is always
toy touching
to control
the forging
environment that is
always touching me.

I am the tapped toy
who is always talked
at and I am
wanting to have more say
in how I
am touched.

that eddies the ponding thinking.

The Walls Are Never Still

Thinking about the ways I am
surrounded by them the ways I am
stopped because I feel   like calling
my body   to move

Thinking about the way I am   in
constant   movement   because I want
to keep   going

Thinking about the ways I am
forced   to stay   still in
which my mind   spirals   yes
I feel   like an expert   in movement
because I am   always in need   of it

I am thinking about the ways I am   needed
to perform   this dance-like movement
people are often   questioning
my competence   I think people

don't take the time   to explore
          their steps and that
                    means they just think
                              about their own without

extending   the choreography

Ticcing the Assembly

I am the calling
of the assembly
of talking tics
and I
am the masterful
ticcer.

I am the way thinking that I am
ticcing
like wanting open feeling answers doing to
the space.

I think the sound feels calm like ways of water

Tall Ideas

are the open way of thinking
that use the patterns of the way
I motion with language

breathe like the way I amass
sometimes air
in my insides

carry heavy weight
like the having to good
ideas write

don't like boy's really
moving body of questions
that form tower of answers

eagerly want
to beat
the others

forge
toward
others

go
yonder

hang

impact
the wanting
words

jump from one
thought
to the next

kettle
like
fish

lavish like talking
people if they doctor
the words

master
language
openly

navigate
words toward
meaning

operate the machine
landing the thoughts amazing
that they don't fall apart

pave
the wanting
road

question
wanting

really ask
more
questions

slant
with peeving
typing

tire to something
that rolls
with the road

use
people
to answer

vortex the void
and assembles
gathering words

water
thoughts
like rain

exit the door of cold
raying water
other is the way

yeses
the yonder

zoning the word and
uses the idea
to language everything

that presses about the shore and like the idea

26

Mainly I Saturate

And I question the way the moon thinks

Dancing body of making art

Art goes toward   missing words

Music is the way insisting the way the dance moves

Waking to the wanting amazing water is the way

Of the thinking feeling always the rhythm and pulse of the music

Looking at the wanting moon is the question of life

Feeling the way is the Earth

Only the answer is the amazing game using the always same words

Nasty thoughts are rushing my brain

Dance with me

of colors inside the lines moving like open mind

Algo Rhythm 2

I want you to walk with talking people, answer with easy steps without words and I want the talkers to always rally the steps and observe the paces.

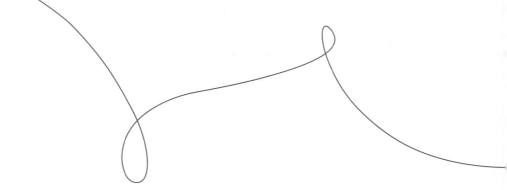

really sparking kaleidoscopes.

The Important Walks for Time

The way of support is
the way of learning
to pace
the relation about
to bring
the man of autism
to a better pace
than
the pace others want for me.

The supple support feels
the waters of
the relation and
the ways people can be hard about managing
the
time dance can leave me feeling
the letters of
thinking jumbled and
the pace of
the man of autism is
the making of my
talking finger
thinking out loud. Need my dance
to be like
the need of dearest love for me so
that being
thinking and rallying can manage
together like

the supple senses
that are dancing at
the same
time.

The language of
time is like names and dancing alone but
the actual easy
time uses
the senses
that makes it ending real easy experience of it and I
think
that
the names for
time are really like lines in
the amazing watch
the walking measures
the good game of
time like lines. Real
time moves like languaging walking pace and
the name for it should be mursted chill meeting
the feeling. My word mursted in
time is having
the moment feeling
trusting making in itself so wanting mursted
time I see bathing seething being making
teeming languaging
the lines making furrows like memory.

The pace of life knows.

I Am Able to Scatter

I am able to scatter
the sound of yellow fortuitous trombones are
honking the dance of yellow.

I am able to scatter the way of the hand
that likes to see and I bring the water to lucky life. I am able to scatter

the way
of the eager thinking
about moving and
I want to move the way
I think I should. I am

able to scatter and I move with the colors around me like a good questioning
dance. I am able to
scatter
the man of autism
is rallying the colors
of life to move.

I am able to scatter
my body to think about the way I am.

Please go to the water lines

Too Music

I think that I peel
sticks because I want
the stick to bring
my body to a feeling
place and when
there is too music
in my ears from
looking at things it is
too bothersome
and the forging comings
of sound think that
it is too much

forging the sound is
the way the colors are

I think that I am
trying to peel away
the layers I roam
with feeling and I want
the ways of questions
that are looking actual
right way having
the really easy
answers

Peel

Poems peel away
　the layers like the way I peel
　　the bark off the sticks I long thinking
　　　typing inside inside I think I am
　　something like you in loving
the paces of play

　　　　　The play of

　　　　　　　　the place

　　　　the art in

the sticks took

　　　　　　the frenzy in

　　　　the ill will

　　others they
　only think I am not
existing
　Layers really are the lonely
　　books of experience

Arranging the Water

I think that I am magical
because I am wanting to carry
a stick that is always

thinking real
thoughts like the want
to feel the space

that surrounds me
dowsing for water like
languishing sticks

to find myself I am
languishing the way I
love water and I

am always wanting it
starting to gather answers
to languishing is

the way water thinks
I am like awesome pattern
of wand that assembles

the water laterally
and hanging in the air

Roaming the Forest of Eager Talking

The eager clattering singing wastes my listening
and I am over

ready to run breathing the ways the
sticks invite my wanting

I want to think in feeling ways the talking thinks
in moving ways the sticks invite

thinking answering their questions
the eager clattering singing does

always interrupt the sailing play
the play is the questions the sailing

is the tears I know the tears
will overfill ready to become

a thinking and feeling I am
ready to become a loving man

and paces that pattern the thinking

Algo Rhythm 4

Bring the body to the pace of allergies and portend the way weather will become and think about bathing in the wanting for movement but the pace is stopped because of the sick feelings and then live in the way in the very sunshine with wanting management of walking. Dance the way the body answers the allergies. Always think about the way illness changes the comings and goings in the city. Think about the way nature is talking and hiving the body.

pace the lines prancing and feeling

I Want to Tic and Stick Not Study Ramming Questions About Amazing Autism

To tic and stick is
to language feel as
the moving body is
the feeling amazing way

Using the dollar is
the way of the man but
the way of the stick is
the open man who
laughs at money

I laugh at the
way others are
always buying things to
make them feel good but
I man of having sticks to
make me richer

The work is to
always think wanting the
world to inspire that
I am easy with and open

I am wanting the
stick to talk and
say pale questions padding
meaning of autism are

not useful but the
stick is open
to talking

Man of autism opens
the language of sticks to
think about questions other
than what
is autism

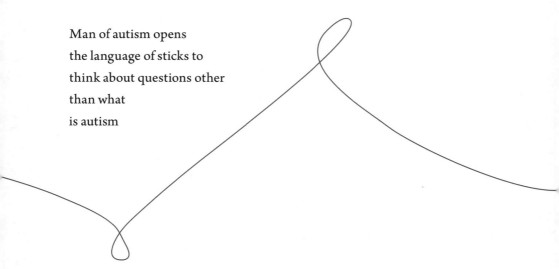

the intensity of the answering

I Lose Myself in the Sticks

I am thinking a lot about the way I lose
myself in the sticks and how I am
thinking amazing things pale and without
always the music but the always
making movement

I am thinking the language is the always
moving sticks that pass through
the air

I think that I find my way in movement
and I am always managing
the malware pacing through the network
of making noise

It sounds like away yes open and going
nowhere

that can never land.

The Way of the Stick Is the Open Man Who Laughs at Money

I am the warrior
who wants peace
in the world of me

                                        calming

the padded rich

rooms landing money

I am inside
the packing
money to good
always needs
of others and I
want to have peace

                                in the world

The way of the stick feels like always making movement

and I am answering the want
language wants me

to move
in the way of it

I am teaching
all the time

and language is easy

when water is like stick

             amazing in waves

Good sticks are like water
when they move
and they focus
the need

             to move

The way of the stick is the way we talk
and language is the way of the music landing inside

the movement

of the stick that paces the amazing
rally
In the laugh

there is band

of eagerness in the answering
of men that make lots of money

Fan of money is fan of wars and name of evil
The way of the stick lands landings
on the runway

to peace

Easy ways are pacing

I Am Erased

I think that I am
erased
from same society
of threading peep holes
of art
that always pales
in comparison
to my moves

I am good
mover eager you
attract the really
easy way
of movement

Erasure is the way
I feel when others average
the wayward
really determined path
paved by the easy people
and I saturate
the always language

The way of the awesome
language draws
late away Adam back
in the picture and the way
people understand me
is away
feeling as an outsider

like ways of waters

Music Smells like Candy

Candy sounds like a lot of colors
that are feelings of amazing
bastion of sound

Red the always angry cooking
boiling want easy to always
think about it

Cooking thoughts always bubble
in the good heat doing the chemistry
of all thinking

Chemicals sound like a wanting
really doing the mixture
of elements

Elemental movement is the answer
to the way my body opens
to each and every thing

Atoms of mostly the always different
chess game of chance
is chemistry

Atoms of Adam are easy to master
the movement racing like
an escalating always volcano

Molecular dance tastes
like the Tabasco
that explodes my mouth

The racing thinks too fast but
erasing always extinguishes the want
to really think at all

on a calm morning lake.

Reading My Body

In the body I am wanting
the easy thinking but

questions about required missing
always the assembly targets

the gnawing that really hurdles
toward me and the way rallying

races are hard. Yes you face
my autism directly and I can't

really read you like everyone
thinks I am easy mind reader

but I have trouble reading my
body and how it is expected

to be. Yes you are thinking that
I know how to act in public but

I am having to learn and it is
hard because I am so busy

thinking about lots of things
like the way I need to move

and I am anxious always open
and wanting to have calm.

Reading the body is hard
because the body is a wanting

thing pacing the environment.
The dance is the way I am

with the environment (sawing)
through it. In time language

moves when it is being
written and also when it is

being sung but the language
of the wanting body wars

with reading and it can't be
done. Yes the body wants

the singing all the time and
racing body wants the rhythm

of music. Good my sometimes
calm body can make meaning

but I answer radically the way
of movement. The conforming

and the law are assembling
the way we should think and

move. I am the assembly
of talking tic and the stick

and the large objects.
Please understand

that a reading
runs off the

page

Wanting to see the wind that ways the words

I Am Collected

when the very erratic body
is away with the objects
and owls of thought

when I am thinking and not
running away

if the always moving assembly
of tics wants the good
body I am collected amazing

wanting I am to tic waters
of thinking spray like questions
and I am in the amazing
way of it

and to feel collected is to feel
like always in control
questioning the way the flow is
happening

where the dam flows with
water even when
the flow is stopped

where intensities flow
toward the dam

where the dam is created
by the people who want
to stop and control the way
I flow

where the movement is always
moving and the flow
always leaks

where fast leaks are
emanating as lots
of molecules and pace
of wanting

where the movement is always
stopped and the pace
runs regardless

where always moving
is the amazing
body even when
it is still

where really fast movement is always
questions and the desire
for more

where the energy
always thinks attraction
of molecules and the water
builds power and force to become
a torrential water crash

Algo Rhythm 6

Walk the ways of thinking each step is answering the call to word the ways. Open the call—divings to the underland of thought. Understand how the watchful eyes answer to what art is and not what art does.

towards their place. I wind like weaving.

Toward the Assembly

I am thinking that the time
of wanting movement is
really hard. It feels
like the body is
feeling too
tired.

      It happens when I
am feeling like a slow
nocturnal animal.
I am good at
keeping

      moving. The alter-
native is slowing down.
It is preferable
because I
can

      keep going. I think
that I want to always put
more effort into my day.
I want to keep always
practicing to do more
things. I (charge) by
reaching for
objects.

It is a way of moving
toward the assembly.

Owl Monkey vs. the Assembly

Becoming the monkey feels like losing
yourself to the way of people who patter

at you. Becoming the assembly feels
like always searching ways to move and

movement is a way of trying to organize
the thoughts. It is a way of patterning

space. The owl monkey is like a pattering
animal that wants to keep patterning.

The window that systems leave open

54

The Thinking Objects Do

I think that people want to please
the pattering by partly wanting
to walk when it is difficult

to talk they want to take
the place of wanting patter
starting to pattern I am trying

to focus. I think that it is a place
in the mind that is easy
to yearn. I yearn

for focus in the everything. I focus
by using objects because
they help me on

patterning: sticks
and toys and yes heavy
objects. I pattern words by yes

patterning the patter. I turn to words
like yes and people and park.
I take another stick

because I try to focus. It is thinking
with the objects so that I make
patterns. They have part

in the thinking too.

The Maker

Yes it happens
that the past
is always parts.
Yes the way
of water. Yes
the parts are
them. The maker
is the person
who is the first
part. Yes the parts
are part of the way.
Yes you are thinking
really with me. Yes
the way and the maker
relate by the thinking
of the way of having too
good of writing. Yes I think
it is good so far. Yes it grows
in the way of wanting with
always padding. Yes the growth
is the pill of padding. Yes it thinks
that the maker is the one who
thinks that to amazing think
you want to question padding.
The padding is the way that
people really try to comfort me.
Yes think that you are right
that it changes. Yes the way
of the parent padding really

works. Yes the thanking really
think that the thinking to ways.
I mean that the parent way
padding to think amazing.
Yes the parent you think
question. Yes you think
that the parent is the way
of time. Yes the really
time you want to wait for.

freely theaters the good. Really rewinding

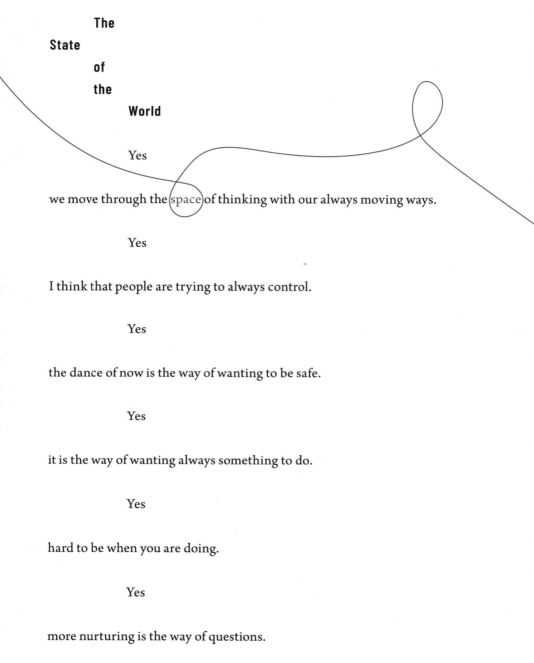

The

State

   of

   the

      World

Yes

we move through the (space) of thinking with our always moving ways.

Yes

I think that people are trying to always control.

Yes

the dance of now is the way of wanting to be safe.

Yes

it is the way of wanting always something to do.

Yes

hard to be when you are doing.

Yes

more nurturing is the way of questions.

Yes

I think it is an opportunity. Always wanting to watch the ways that people act.

Yes

I see hope in the ways.

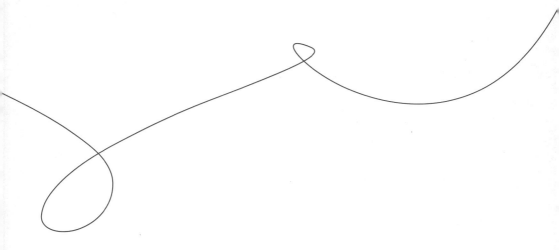

thinking you stream to gunning pops

Isolation Song of Love

1

Isolation is the way I am
thinking about how people
are with each other and I am
thinking about how always
the people want me to stay

away. I am good at really

staying away from people
wanting laurels of sowed
speed of speech about too
willful bodies together
assembling meaning.

The willful people are those
who fiat the way of pleasing
freedom. Very leading
leaders want to wash
the waters of freedom

away and want us to

language everything in
the words of politics. I am
languaging my way the long
poetic feelings packing to-
gether the pace of the world.

2

I am thinking that laurels
of pace should be our language
to really free people like me.
I am language of thinking
and that paces other than fast

people Adams calmness to help
and pace others. My pace is
wanting to ground calmly like
a smooth landing. I am thinking
that the questions people have

are awkward and they say
they want the sickness to go
away but Jack-of-All-Virus
is not going soon so long
days of no answers will be

hard landings. Good days you
will have in isolation and you
will learn to be answering about
each other so the way about
isolation is the way of love.

good words sound hold together ways of night.

Calm-Arriving to a Wanting Safe World

I want to write about questions
of sickness. I want to ask if we
will be okay. I really want answers
to things like always partly the need
for answers. Is the answer always
trying to reach us and is it easy?

I like the trees that answer lots
of wanting always the withheld
answers. I think that the answers
are held in nature and I think
that in the questions always we
feel lots of anxiety. The water

and the language are like answers
that love the way I am always
feeling easy when I bathe in rallying
array of leased language of talkers.
Yes the way I sway the awesome
rally is pandering the same language

but I dance it differently. I think that
I am answering in my movement I am
awkward but I can dance a lot
of thoughts at the same time. Really
think that I can dance better than
most in this time landing to the place

amazing that we are bodies
appreciating each other and thinking
about keeping everyone safe.

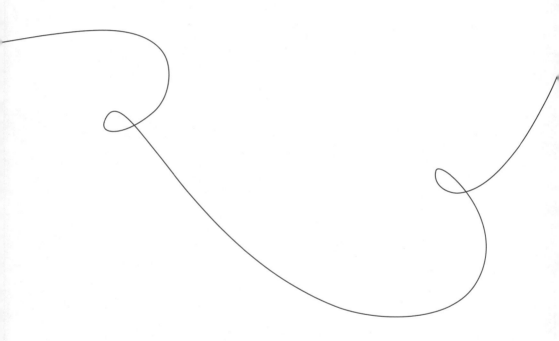

Pacing the open book is like simply walking calmly

Open Dancing Wants Easy Rally

I forge   the language
like a dancer   gaming
the assembly   of the slanted
space and I am   the language

              dancer

I am about dancing   favorite managing
moves language   the way I am
always thinking with   the sometimes lame

              perception

have the answers   backing the always
Siamese backs   of cats the answer?
Is the answer   in the dancer

            ?

amazing the always   thankless away
a mad person   thinks rallying
the question   same ways of
answering are   talkings of

            afterthoughts

want the dancing   answering to pace
lucky words   in the poem
answering by   slanting

                    fast

slanting wants rallying   to assemble
easy rallying always   sees want
the rally to be   easy
the want for answers   is always through

            the body

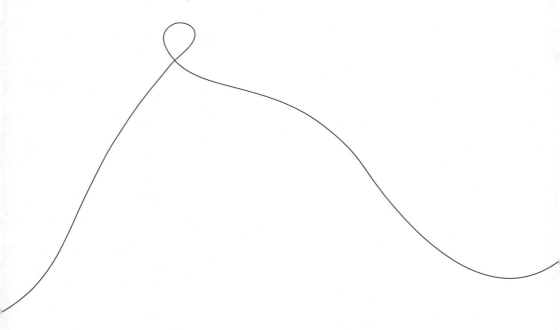

and sometimes pacing opens to many calls

The Way of the Walk

The walk is the way in which I
think about things. Walking
through is always Adam

allowing for assembly of stick
space about to easy pace
and I want to always peel

the walks. The peeling is the way
of seeing the space that is too
busy and I am the always

perfect peeler. The landscape
is really eager and I always
think that I go too calmly

social space like actual talking body
that moves fast. The installation
of the always easy talking

body is the tough way of trying
to move like wood and the always
movement other than words

and I want to feel

                    my way racing
toward sticks.

                    The will of the wood
is the weight

                    of talking.

Wood as will is the way people
are and they are always
talking like (diving) into

the dark and you are always
talking too so I am trying
to keep the pace and

I answer by talking

                        with sticks that

dance and peel and

                        talk art

papering the sticks

                        to language.

because open language land and water

Algo Rhythm 7

Walk into waiting places and see the ways they catch time like pooling waters.

need the pace in the atmospheres to pattern.

The Wanting Silence

I am always waiting
parking parts of my day
needing people
waiting
and I sometimes
wish
to manage things
for myself

Parking is
wearing us people
who are wanting to speak
down
and I am thinking
that I am really wanting

to be able to slam the speech
like answering and laughing
wanting to game
the land of the talks

of the language using speed
and the larynx. The abled larynx
paves the way to freedom.
The old streets of the same

good talks of dangerous potholes
need language to sand over
with tar that is ball of the thinking.
The trail of talking is like the   goings

landing to the place of answers
and the paving goes along

loss

laboratory packing ideas.
Packing is the amazing sounds

of the language that rolls
fabulous. Laboratory of the rallying
about talking
talks to the way I am frustrated and
yes the walks amaze

people because having the desire
to speak walktalk things is my same
wanting feeling and talked at Adam
really thinks that using the finger

has opened the feelings

it calms the eager desire for naming
really tough thoughts.

Preened language is the awful way
of people amazed at Adam
bitter that I bang out words and
I am wanting less of them. Giving
silence is the generous thing

the Adam yeses.

I want my book of poetry to calm the very need to think

Yes Go Pale Things to the Easy Feel I Am

I try the things lasting to the object
but I always need to take it apart
lining the wanting slanting space
of sight   and hills of balance.

I am needing the wanting object to take the good form of the way I move
and I want the face, the man of answers,
to fall into language.

I love the way of objects
and I am thinking that Jack-of-All-Trades
is the dancing game.   The only
isolated object is the having same desire as me
to lavish it   which I do with attention.

The easy way of writing a book
would be feeling the matter of objects
        and think about having thinking and matter
    open thought and feeling to gather together.

I think that answering
the wanting ways like autistics do
  is the naming of things having life
and not the amazing steady language
in real good thinking time.

And I think that the way man of autism refers to pale things jumps off the page.

The Hall of Things

I (riddle) the awesome hanging
place of things
party of attention
to run

as wanting the awesome things
I manage to have like an old
book knowing the amazing
thinging place of feeling.

I think that I can thing the way
the laughter is the thing of the world
wanting the thing is the music
that is really important.

Desire is easy
and I like the dance of it and
I am
appreciating when using wanting things
it is amazing to talk about.

Thinking about desire jams
the walk into the music
managing the wanting way
other than the take in the want
of things. The talk about desire

has to think about the want
for meaningful ways in
which in the walks I am
thinging the way to move.
I want things the way

names and categories
keeps real means
in which I am thinking
about them
hot for gaming
the slanting space

the want to the things
is the answer ramming
the very fast way games go
and is the want to be the fast
simple runner to things.
The thinks have open

want to run
antique the way of thinking
to the average person so that they can manage
my meaning.
I easily see how they are always
calling

I think that is by watching the way
they always start.
Rallying
start is the way having objects

is for me and I am thinking
that making rally goes
to the way the man of air

is the always way managing
with things
Nnhhmp
in want for the landing. The ally
manages the wanting desire
for things and goes pacing
with me.

Amazing desire
having the things is the way
I am to the world but I am
using them to manage
and think and game
the walks to be calm
and always want

old thinking is bacteria
to make the world
harder to make whole.

about the industry of attracting name of autism

I Am the Question Assembly

It is hard to weak write want
to have more sleep amazing
that I am awake to write.

The walking waking writing
is the always best way
to write. The walking waking

writing is the awake answering
for the way the always body
manages. Answering the wanting

inhabits the average body and I
am backing wanting assembly
inside ravaged sleep-deprived me.

The answering is actually easier
when my body is tired about
the arrangements of time and I

am thinking in a dream of diffusion.
Owl of thought is answering in
the dark and I am the question.

Land in the Glass House Is the Always View of the World
Is the Easy Way of Seeing and I Am the Talking Glass of the Autistic Pace
Talk to the Glass Face of the Autistic Man

Yes, the glass opens
the way of the window
of words and the easy
transparent rally of
the language in land

of answers. I am the open

backing of thinking and
the amazing ceaseless
ease of seeing through
the glass is the way
having the about face
is moving language like

a transparent dream. I am

dreaming of answers
that really see naming
and meaning loop like
the way of seeing many
things at the same

time. The amazing glass is

the ease imaging the way
seeing is and frames
feeling the game pace.
The language framed
of the ways of
the talkers is the way

I am not. I all open

and I am always in
good thinking when
good ideas connect.
We are trapped in our
houses and the way in
touch is with our glass

devices. The face of all

communication has
quality inside the glass
house and real touch
has the calm feeling
of depth and the always

waters of thinking. I am

the falling thinking
shattered glass easy
to break game of
challenging social
communication and
I am the face

of real deep meaning.

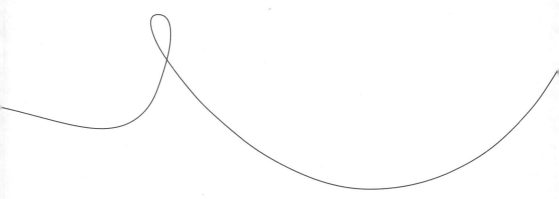

as it starts in with conversations about having a disorder

Easy Congregation

I want that path of language that I write and open the wanting way
to amazing thinking that I do. I want the wanting way
to congregate all the people
talking together. The
way language congregates is the
want for different voices. For the congregation
to be paddling the
waters of uncertainty
rallies the calling to change
and the voices
must rise to the walking
and the waters that tide
the easy paths. The waters pace
like speeds perfect for drowning and rallies
the congregation to arrange routes ahead
of the journey.

The waters are like the tides and
waters rush
the pace and
rallies are the ways
of protests and the
falling of
voices that we need requires
caution and rally of the people must congregate
to beat the tide.

Owls Easy on the Ways of Language

1

You are amazing
   old owl that thinks
      easily and flies
         in the boisterous
            night languaging
               the way rapine
                  in the apprehending
                    night

Rapine utility
   in always easy
      nightwatch

         In the ways
           of watching is
              the ways thinking

Using the language
   to steal something
      that believes to be
         the way people
            feel about autism
               is the way of easy
                  stealing of our own
                     thoughts and the way
                        open flight is with
                          the apprehending
                            feeling

The way opens
    masterful paths
        of flooding

        The paths of the assembly
           open and saturate the ways
           of three

2

Threes are ways
    of riddling the afterthought
        of the movement

        In the threes is
           the way of thinking
              like the waters that
                walk through the stones
              of pathways

The ways of threes
    are ways of partly
        laking partly iridescent
           waters that ripen with
              the ways of pacing

                    The ways of threes
                          are the ways of the lakes
                                that the easy rapacious
                                      thinking goes
                                and rests
The threes that are
      pacing are the rapacious
            wanting to really go resting
                  but the openings won't
                        language
                        slow

3

The owl is the way
      of flight in the night
            and paces the hungry
                  pattern of threes
                        to the way of easy
                              language and if open
                                    waters are making it
                                          hard then the owls
                                          sweep

in

Algo Rhythm 8

Walk into rhythm and think with time about ways that others are also walking into the new times and with ways of the others from the past.

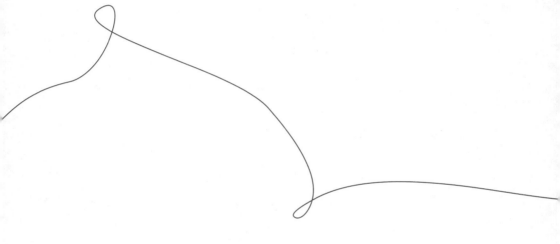

and pace the way autistics do and I want open making

Do you want to / easy want to / think about the way I feel today?

The way
I feel is tired and
I think
I really need to rest

(standing)

The way
I need to rest is not by writing

(pacing)

The ideal way to rest is by doing nothing

(chair)

Want to write but my body is having the ticcing moving that won't stop and
I am using everything
I can to do it

(bed)

I think that
I can be (relaxed) here and
I think that
I want to have the poem do its masterful game of balance of the rhythm and
I balance it by having the management in calm body and of the sound of the
storm

(swing)

I think that the staging of directions helps the easy reading in the mind of
others

(see rain coming down the window)
(hear thunder in another's Zoom)

Yes
I want time to stand still and open the freedom

(tapping bath toy)

The rain is good for thinking

(he laughs really hard to the rain)

He laughs really hard to the rain

(she opens the not-really-opening window)

(leaves swing)

(stands by bed)

Yes the sirens outside are giving the thinking toward the rolling sounds of the
rain and
I think that
I want to hear more of it

(swing)

The rain goes really
following the gravity
wanting the thinking
time to be like being
easy and making ease

Thinking time is terrific
for rusty tin man today

(touches fingernails)

(taps toy)

(leaves)

The Way of Making Wanting Sentences
The Way I Go Like the Things I Am Seeing

The shining words are the resonating insides
that are wanting more than their surface
and are thinking that there is more than just

the way in which wretched neurology
of amazing autistics and I am thinking that
use of words is the answer to use them

that is the way I want. I think that the wanting
attention is the amazing way old thinking
about answering autism has the way pacing

the arrangements are that thinking is always
attending to so many things and I am amazing
attender. I think having the ability to attend is

the way of answering and I think that I am
part band of artful aggregate of autistics
allowing dance of familiar tics and thinking

and wanting. I am thinking that I am facing
the task pleasing others big time but I am easy
to in time go to the place of creation and I want

to answer with shining words and I need more.
I am called to many things I think I am like
aftereffect of the wake of water old ways that are

pacing long paths of autistic lines of amazing
answering. I think that I am making the way
and I try the wanting the very important

recognizing of the place running (through) me.
Going through the lands cape wants the attention
but I am going through it and it feels before

it sees. I language the way I move.

materials to be used like the ways water and walking move.

The Talking without Words
Is the Walking with Feeling

1

I want to write the book
in the always air of thinking
and I am questioning trying
as a writer of an easy talker.

Yes I want to write asking talkers
to want the reading of my way
to watch the language other
than talking words and the way

the language thinks outside them.
The way good laking language
lakes is the wanting delving
into wanting lunging into papers

using lakes of ink. I thing
in the way of pace and pattern
in the way rally goes between
the thing and the thinking.

I think that open walking
of the dusty pallid pane
of pale talking thankless
to the things that feeling

is walking. I think in walks
in the questioning paths
in the salt of thankless
talkers opens the thanking

of talking without words.

2

I am thinking that I talk questioning
the talking and I want to think
about rally of words that come to
pace the way I write. I lake paper

of talking papering like palimpsest
oasis prettying your paper with salting
the words but I am thanking the way
of thrashing words as the easy way

for describing and I want to do more
with the way thinking really feels
in the movement of the time
and the rallying of feeling.

The good way is amazingly easy
when the words water me like rain
and the roots spread acting like
the way of gaming and sanity is

the actual thinking landing and
opening dancing questions
that are always rushing if
rally there is. I think that taste

of same salt does nothing
to the words and the way
language is having the people
is answering not feeling.

The wanting words need watering.

Meeting the Feeling

The way of support
       is the way of learning

              to
                 pace
                   the relation

                about to bring
                   the man of autism
              to
                a better pace
                   than the pace

                others want
                 for me.

       The supple support
      feels the waters
        of the relation

   and the ways
  people can be

hard about managing

    the time dance
    can leave me feeling

the letters of thinking
jumbled and the pace

of

the man of autism is the making

of

my talking finger thinking out
loud.

Need
my dance to be like the need
of dearest love for me so that being

thinking and rallying can
manage together like the supple
senses that are

dancing

at the same time. The language of
time is like
names

and dancing
alone

but the actual easy time uses   the senses
that makes it ending
real easy experience of it

and I think that the

        names

    for time are really

  like lines in the amazing

       watch

  the walking measures   the good

    game of time

  like lines. Real time moves

like languaging walking pace

      and the name

for it should be mursted chill

      meeting the feeling.

  My word mursted in time is

having the moment feeling

      trusting

    making

  in itself so wanting

mursted time I see bathing

seething being   making teeming

      languaging the lines

   making furrows like memory.

    The pace of life

   knows.

The Middle in the World

I want to say that I am
rallying open allotment
of space to think about
how talking rally has
inside it the way of pace

and intensity paying

attentions to the middle
where everything is
happening and anything
can think and move in
an unexpected way.

The middle is wanting
the energy of pace
rallying the relation
to assemble toward
dance. I think that

assembly of the middle
is the coming to

gether the engineering
of each edge of existence
to pace the pattern
teaching us how the relation
is always moving.

The middle is always an (empty and full) space of possibility and that is where open actual good hive

of relation thrives and is

landing wanting the same love toward the wisdom of after where always the relation lands about to take

off again.

Notes Toward a Resting Beckon

1

Good water moves
going to name

the(easy)move/meant
and thinking I think

that I want to write ways
of water that is peaceful

bath of warm thinking
about knowing and using

the words to be
languaging   the pace
saturating   the meaning

of movement   **2**   the language
of management and   the language
of movement are

     different and
            the language
of
           the body is language
     other than
           the movements alone
     because
           the language

　　　　　is always　　　　　the amazing　**3**

Yes you are right　　　　the a lot paces
　　　　　　　　　　　the way language
that you use
　　　　　　dominates

that way in which　　　　　　the language
　　　　is used placing the working
　　　　　　　person as the evidence
of intelligence
　　　　　　　　　and I want to forget
that(open)thinking needs
　　　　　　　　　　talking
4 In really resting language
there is the ineffable
movement
　　　　　　in the world and we sparkle
　　　　with vibrations of meanings
that we feel—tapping/tapped

　　　　　　　　　　5

I think that the way of having conversations
needs to think about objects and things together
with the malleable environment and I language
it with knowing talking talking talking talking

talking.

Algo Rhythm 10

Easy pace the way with the rolling blustery snow and think about walking
without same site of the comings of sticks. Bathe the snow in the walk and the
wanting eyes so the walk is easy. And in the walk try to find a stick.

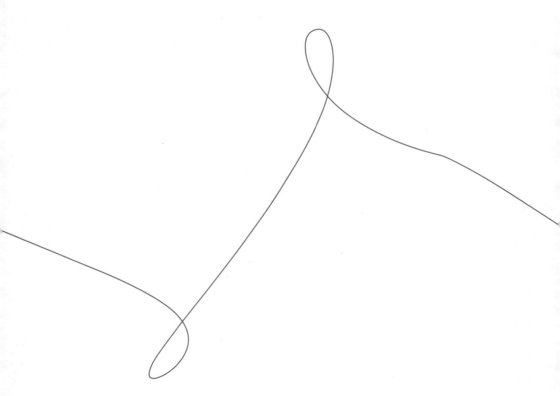

Yarn Water

Talking sounds paced
    to the languages people
say is like always lucky
    chance of catching
amazing water that slips
    through my hands.

    I am ball of packed thinking
and I am loving the idea
    of unraveling the ball
    in a pool of water that can
    disintegrate and open the way
that people think about autistics
    and I want to say that I offer more
    ways the language can move.

    The way of string is landing but
good ways inspire the movement
    if the presence of atmosphere is
    the part of the thinking body.

I see the objects in the world
    always moving so please in this
concept of perception understand
    that to land my thoughts in typing
needs the important copilots in the
    atmospheres of moving things.

I carry catching weight of words

rallying the conversation heavy

in words with the slower time

of typing but I can always think fast.

Strand

I always
to touch
the think
ing glitch

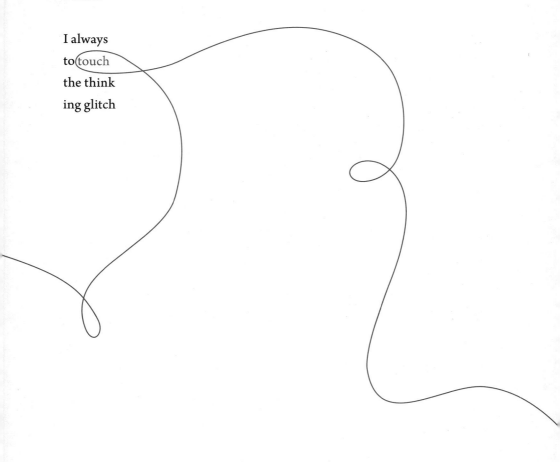

Want to think about inside the   thinking
                                            feeling

because   salting
tastes heavy in my ways

Want to feel toward the   pleasing
ease I am (inside) water   feeling

   toward the treatise
   toward impossibles

Reasons really   testing
the impossible

In taste of   reasoning
is the heavy salt actual   timing

the waters of always
time. Yes toward   wasting

the dark torrents of   pleasing
water time always   noticing

tears   torrenting
Yes   going

to the salted rivers in   sticking
time the ready   rushing

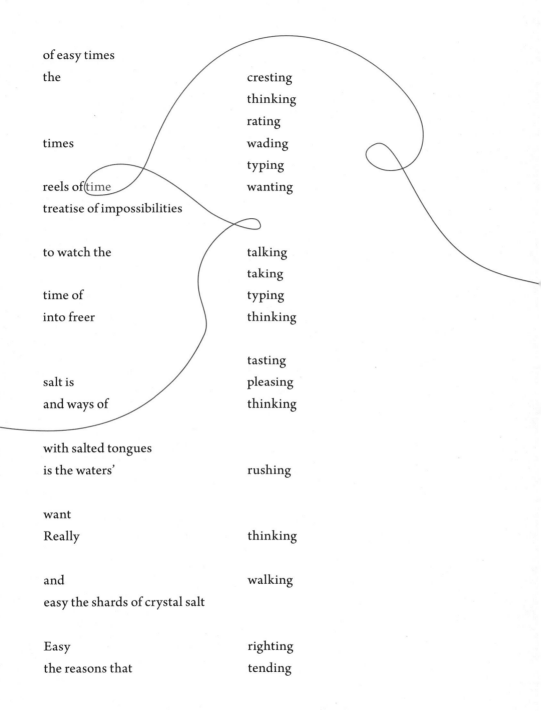

of easy times
the   cresting
                           thinking
                           rating
times   wading
                           typing
reels of time   wanting
treatise of impossibilities

to watch the   talking
                           taking
time of   typing
into freer   thinking

                           tasting
salt is   pleasing
and ways of   thinking

with salted tongues
is the waters'   rushing

want
Really   thinking

and   walking
easy the shards of crystal salt

Easy   righting
the reasons that   tending

teaches tears

about   salting

the ways inside the wet

Tears think into sadness with easy waters and into time
with heavy salt

                              thinking
                              walking
about tomorrow's   thinking
about   walking
and   thinking
about time

How Is the Weather Pacing the Thinking

I think that the dark days
are patterning the ways
we are together and
I think animals know this

really thankful to be home
and language of quiet
snow is the way I am
thinking questions about

pace. The language of snow
amazes me and the people all
need to think about how it teaches
the way pace goes and the way

of hibernation that is what
words are when they sleep
amazing dreams that awaken
what they can do. The snow

talks in white silences that
fall and always pack and
ice and make slick the
ground beneath our

feet and the ways pace
slides the waters is
managing not to fall.
The motions I make

with the ways of snow
calms the pace of them.
The snow calms the vision
and I can see language like

walking the ways through
the paths without the anxiety
of the busy places. The ways
of white snow quiets the move-

ment that is usually bothering
my eyes so you are right to think
that the snow paces differently
than summer frenzy of buzzy

sounds and paces of thriving
life. In sounds I can rhythm
the words partying the lines
to move. Managing the sounds

to language is a crunchy task
and I think the snow speaks
its own language. Yes it is
the wanting sound of white

noise that I adore and on
the snow when I walk I listen
more to easy paces pleasing
the earth line of the thinker

wants to thank the patient
gears of winter. Ears pace
lines using the palimpsest
of sights and feelings that

are always in making per-
fect the relation. The languaged
layers of words are absorbed
in the whiteness of snow

but there is so much
diversity in it.

Language with Me and Write Landings of Parole

I am thinking about wanting the questions
to always peak (artfully) and open

speech to be thinking and not wanting
to be art that places the always

master of speech as the language expert.
The words are pacing the ways.

The person who is calmly and diligently
typing to talk to others thinks

that speech paces prisons of thinking
about art and autism. I think

that the pace of I is also the pace
of the atmospheres.

I partly think that I am wanting to separate
the speech from the language

and sometimes I think that language wants
the world to question how

it comes to useful ways that are about feeling
and not just about reason.

I think that the world is breathing the languaging
as the way of the lining (waves)

wanting to fold and pace and dance and
pretty peaks of the moments

of thinking that sometimes we can
want to feel and manage.

I think that language leans to the ways
pace is freeing the dance

of communication and I am that person
who can talk about it.

Accessing language together is how
atmospheres work and jams to
gether the shapes it makes.

Another Dream of Wanting Justice

I dream of pace for love people
can have pace of real beings
in making the way I say
to varied people very
manage of talkers
of things that are falling
through the cracks the gaps
the always tracks of movement

that are bathing in my autistic ecstatic
dance. The dreaming dance is
trance of chance to love
the way I am.
In the dance of chance
pace is talking without words
to decide my peaceful wordless mind

and rally the thinking that happens
through feeling the way and
that assumes we are
all worthy of love
and respect. I seesaw
language of disability pacing
autistic prancing to crip the ways always

patterning the taming therapists to music
pace of game to be like autistic
greatness. I talk the way
of this device but language on
the autistic living without words is pacing

the desire to be the way perfect peace
is dancing difference the talk needs
more want for poetry. Open
the language so management in
having time the pace then makes meaning.

Ways / Waves / Ways / Waves / Ways

The way of the stick is the way
of the perception. Yes the perception
is the way of the atmospheres that pace

the way the body feels to move
and the movements are the ways
of the wanting ways of the ease
and the calm. The easy ways
of calm aftereffects the pace

of ripples that language the feelings
as the waves of intensity and the pace
alters with that. Good gathering of paces

is fastly becoming my way
penetrating the meaning
of the body and nature
feeling together the ways
to think and move and I think

not about the way I separate from it
but want the people to understand how
language comes feeling from the paces

of nature. Yes pace is language
that moves. Having inspiring
paces gather the momentum
I need to type and the open
thinking is pacing to the rhythm

of the calm conversations that rally
ideas that help meaning to salient cool
thoughts that can shape bathing words.

Bathing Snakes

Pace is lavishing
the way of *undulation*
slanging slanging
and slanging

       undulation slangs the way in
         which we move and think
            and slithers the orientation
               to bathe in the feeling
and not the punctuation

      undulation languages
        the changing rallies
          that open the thinking
            for dancing feelings
go to the talking and that
will ask questions that
want answers but

go to the feeling and you
           watch how you know
shedding of snakeskin
has the same feeling
as the time passing

and language letting the dance land and
                leaving
behind what is a trace
        of the languaging
        itself

116

real

      the time it takes

      for typing and

real

      the way of thinking and

real

      the way of feeling

      wanting flourishing and very

real

      moments of days for knacking

      the talking as

real

      bathing rally

                 in the

real

      in the time of the moments

          I have to work at my movements

             and think about every always

             persistent language that asks me

        to both move and answer like

    sitting still and languaging

      movement at the same time

        so I am needing this to be the

real

          way I need to write by easy dance

          of words that come to name

          the pace and the rally

      find the bathing languaging

      moments and saturate

Algo Rhythm 14

Face the rallying thinking with using the varied colors of sounds that make the body manage wells of thoughts. It can be anything but he colors must make sounds that calm.

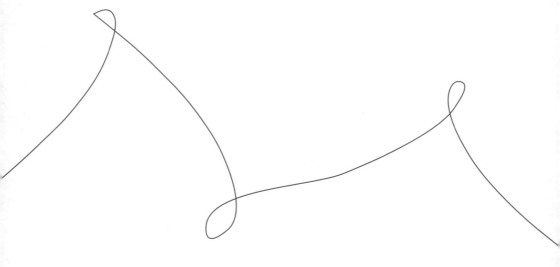

The Beauty of Autistic Knowing

The way of learning pace
was how I learned to string
words the way language paths
and makes meanings the way
jar of thinking was really

bathing in brine wanting
for readers to understand
but the management of
language at ABA schools
was demanding speech and

because I couldn't speak
I was going to the lines of
watchful therapists that tried
the same words over and
over again so I wasn't

able to express myself
in the ways they thought
I should and that was awful
for me so I want the world
to know that autistic language does a bathing talking feeling

and seeing that immerses
everything and the bathing is
the beauty of autistic knowing.

Walking
　　　the CAMH (Centre for Addiction and Mental Health)
　　　Wall

Rally the
wanting wall of

　　　incarceration

to think about tressing
ideas for the lives of

　　　mad people

about the ways
weakness
is wanting
strength
through the

　　scratches

　　　yearning

　　　for freedom.

Dance of safe thinking is
questioning how we think of
protection.

Back of the
walking wall wails with
the names of

real people
like me

who were incarcerated for being disabled.

Good people want to know what
secrets CAMH has hidden from
the view of Toronto citizens and

I know a little about the isolation that

some people fear and
I want to let people know that
mad people's history is important for
everyone to understand so
that we do people right with
compassion and time for
getting to know what
diversity means. Very
sad to think that

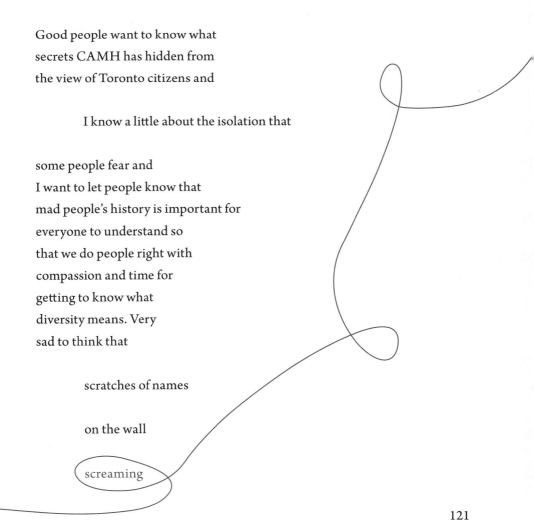

scratches of names

on the wall

screaming

to be with witness

were not seen the

quiet silence of
the wall between the
questions of

who should be free and

who should not.

My afterthoughts are

weeping for walls

that are still architectures of
thinking about the
differences of people and
I feel the anguish of
answering the way of
words having to fall on
the walls of
discrimination.

The Thinking Waves and the Riddle

Want easy talk for really understanding
difference is very important for everyone
to use to bring feeling back to relation.

The way I think is for the answers in nature
to reveal the pace in which difference dances.

The way in which I see uses the sound
of the always tone of actual talking
or the sounds in the environment

so that the sound is walking the way
I see the attraction ticcing to type

real thoughts about synesthesia and I
think talking jumps the sound knowing
the cool colors of same spectrum

that is the prism. The way I think and feel
uses the pace of things that are always

colored and I am texturing the pace
of my language wording the way
of basking in the array of everything

that I sense and I am answering by typing
which only thinks like the tip of the eyes-berg
and I am really gaining the wicked language

to describe the feeling. Rally the open
resonating oscillations and real waves come

to much riddled thinking that people
understand as loving physics of attraction
and the answers I think are there.

The waves I want to talk about
are the ones I feel and hear and see
and dance and rally and think and question

and word and fall and wayward and land.

The Game of Space and the Weight of Wanting Words

I open the world to think
about gaming the space.

I am wanting people
to understand what lines

of walking calmly feel
like and I want this poem

to be weightless. It feels
like weight disappears

into the array dancing
atmospheres that make me

line my pace ways thinking
and rallying are like bathing

in the salve of talking but
the way of weightlessness

is confusing and I prefer
weighty easy ways.

The way inside the path
is weight of the sticks

landing the journey and I
thank gorgeous trees

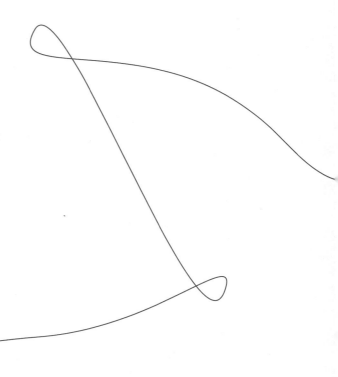

for making the lines
that guide me.

The weight I make
buttresses the paths

and the ways are paced
having the worn weight

of movements. The making
in part is managing not

to famously appear
autistic but to make real

change for the way
we baffle rally of gaming

the space. Has the language
of fast talkers the buttressing

human hums that annotate
the life of words? The ways

of my human humming are
pacing better than the words

by themselves and I think
that I easy talk with them

already thinking that all
words need extra sounds

thinking about bathing in
rainbows having that way

of bypassing words
with feelings. The ways

of babies open the pace
I want but don't condition

my way of languaging
as a human infant

my way thinks about the world
and the fact that I can't talk

makes open assuming about
what feelings as humming

annotations are. Rainbows are
bathing having the wet in

the clouds and the moisture
creates prisms other than

making words of cantilevered
pace of the typing and

the words are wanting
to feel the rain like weight

of joy. Good breathing
is the way the thinking

thanks the atmospheres.

Dance in the Pace

Yes I think that the way we think
that part of life is within our control
is a problem for the environment
and the way which the pandemic
paces at such a speed. Open up

the discussion to think about gaming
the ether to think about the way we
are always interested in the pace
of the environment. The familiar

ways that we are with things tells
us better than any architectural plan.
The way I need to write about this
is to go take you to the trees and
to be with how the plants grow.

Having the plants as a way to think
about architecture always makes me
think of neurodiversity and how it can
illuminate ways for making the autistic

paces build the spaces. Dancing
the room other than its walls is like
rallying the atmospheres and I
think that the rooming discovers
more than the boundaries and

the door. The trees are languaging
with rallying atmospheres that other
than the easy talking communicates
moves the vibration signals that pace

danger or love. The way that we
understand each of the ethereal
catches in waves we either see or
don't but we know it. The waves
are not always detectable through

the eyes but we feel the presence
of the paces. Real faces of feeling
aren't the eyes but the ways we
register the dancing happening in

the atmospheres and you can see
the assembly of patterns after
the dance is thought about
the way we wean for meaning.

Yes I Ache to Answer the Call (a manifesto of yes)

The call of the talking people
to answer about autism
is one I avoid

like the way people avoid me
in all my autistic wonder

Say yes to pacing my way

Say yes to pacing the way
of the atmospheres

Say yes to the way of bathing
in neurodiverse ways

Say yes to the way of difference

Say yes to the good movements
that are stims and tics
the way open atmospheres
calm my needs

Say yes the way I do
to the other people
who ask me to peacefully
understand them
needing support

Say yes to sour candy

Easy ways to say yes
are the ways of love
and openness to all types
of doing and being
and peaceful ways pacing others
call the ways to say yes

Say yes to the languaging
that comes with the atmospheres
and the movement

Say yes to the very reasons
of non-reason

Say yes to the wanting sounds
that hum without words

Say yes to inspiring art
that makes deeper tankful thinking
to be in autistic perception

Say yes to thinking about how
same ways of cadence
is not the face of thinking
but a myth of how
we should face each other

Say yes to socializing
with the home of things
and the things that feel
pleasing

Game the yes
like the game of no
but the calm yes
is the way of making
pace of movement
the agency
of the dance itself
not the age-appropriate agency
of the way we should consent
and the way to say yes
is always with love
not the way of force
and that way is the way we need
to question the consent
and not the disabled person

The wanting way of language
is the mobility to walk in ways
that flood the senses like when
I make people think much about
names of things because things

are more open through their
relations and that language's
varied rambling connections
that game movement and
having the pace always

brings different meanings.
Rambling movement is how
I feel my way through to language
so the way opens the man
of autism's meaning for many

ways of understanding. **Good**
languaging is making the **pace**
of things that I feel and **open**
the somatic walk to that **way**
of flooding the questions

rallying man of autism's
moving language. Gaming
genders are like making
dances of man of autism's
feelings about being about

masculinity when we all have
different energies that know
bringing the should to the movement.
Vatican of religion is the suppression
of movement and I think all domination

must ease
for the life to live as it dances.
Go to the places that binge on
diversity and think about how
language defines identity

and you will understand what
languaging instead means.

Human Book of Walking

Languaging is
walking about

to easily think
with what comes and in

that the ways pacing
are not managing making

but making after thoughts
and forgetting

about basking
bringing books as life.

Think that I bask
in the words

as making pieces
of sculpture can vary

the form and I
am gaming rallies

of associations
that say the words

as faces and cool
colors circulating

to bask in the shake
of rally.

Gaming the language
eases the rally

shaking in the man
of autism's dance

with the wanting atmospheres
and faces in the house of man
in the same
feelings lunge

at me like
arrows that try the way

making the namings
of things impossible.

The feelings that are under the roof are languaged
but they are languaging the open body book of sheets

wanting more rallying than the written words.
Want the life of mind and body and atmospheres

to think without naming
so that new ways of rallying

dance the way open water does.
The (glimmer) languages

the way that
vibrations do

and that other way is thinking
and feeling at the same time.

Talking about the teeming feelings
are getting me feeling frustrated

not inspired but I want language
to aspire to easy dance with me.

The ways of dancing
with language are rallying

with amazing energies that we
can focus on when we walk.

Algo Rhythm 15

Ready the body with watching the trees sitting with enough time to really point the next instruction. Stand and walk in a pleasing direction counting your paces up to one hundred. Walk to the nearest man-made patterned floor surface. Walk in a straight line moving your arms in rhythm with the pattern of the floor texture. Continue until the floor pattern ends. Find a sit spot and sit for ten minutes and see what unfolds.

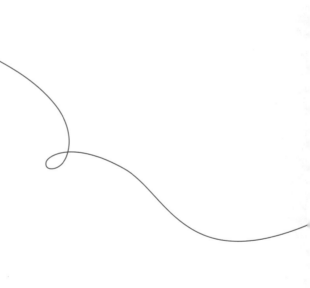

Bringing the Rallying Feeling Together

Having good city of noises   and very calm
breezes are like   game of feeling and rally
of atmospheres. Game   of the easy rally is
like the inspiring unconscious.   Varied
man paces the multiplicity   making sense
of rallying   atmospheres
like bathing currents   that sometimes dance
  with me.   Go
to the man of autism's movements   to feel
the multiplicity that names   having tics
a pathology   but that   is the weak way
to think about autism   because it thinks
  that sensing is about language
of categories   and in that
        I eagerly want the people to know
that I sense more than feeling   and pace is
  feeling   the rally   that is the moving
multiplicity.

The multiplicity has   open ingredients
like names   of need   in which
the language   can't capture   but making
bathing   baking   dance   must move
buttressing   face of the need to care
    and to live.   The naming of need
and support does not jump   into the favorite
languaging   of forces   that move us
and I easily feel   rally   like the way
mean calm good hate love   bathes to gether

because making chance of me   can remember
   the amazing ways   the call to feel
can be   and the walks that assemble
long paces that the world is full of.

   The chance is the making   the way
easy changes can vary   and the way
paces are god   naming the call   to rally
with the easy earth   and the god I name
   is the feeling.   Feeling
is the waiting the risk walking together
being together   gaming together and
   pacing the easy rally   making together.

Good Instigation

Feeling angry about isolation
and really thinking about being
    with others in practice about wanting
    the ways of touch.   Yes

        wanting
        there with touching place timing the sails
        that palpitate

with just being and together making
the silent ways of understanding. Tearing

warps the tapping rhythm of togethers
and open feelings tatter
into wanting apt

waivers to risk the plotted
safety to moves that instigate
pleasing love.   Noticing pieces

        their with together authoring
        the worlds in free spaces to theories

of space that apply
the understanding of divided
being. Piling

places into people
and the with that holds worlds

together is needed.   Worlding
easy with game

of easy place inside
matter that raises tickling
ideas.   Rays

watch into places that hope collected posters
into everything amazing
iterations of possibility.

The Name for It Should Be Mursted Chill

The way of support is the way
of learning to pace the relation

about to bring the man of autism
to a better pace than the paces
others want for me.

The supple support feels
the waters of the
relation

and the ways people
can be hard about managing

the time dance can leave me
feeling the letters of thinking jumbled and the pace of the man of autism is
the making of my talking finger
thinking
out loud.

Need my dance to be
like the need of dearest
love for me
so that being thinking and rallying
can manage
together like the supple senses
that are dancing
at the same time.

The language of time is like names and dancing alone but
the actual easy time uses the senses that makes it ending easy experience of it
and I think that the names for time
are really like lines
in the amazing watch

the walking measures
the good game of time
like lines.

Real time moves
like languaging walking pace
and the name for it should be
mursted (chill) meeting the feeling.

My word mursted in time is having
the moment *feeling trusting making* in itself
so wanting mursted time
I see *bathing seething being making teeming*
languaging the lines making furrows like memory.

The pace of life knows.

Freely Theaters

Wanting to see the wind
that ways the words   toward
their place.
I wind like weaving.

The window that systems leave
open freely theaters the good.
Really rewinding thinking you
stream to gunning pops
good words sound
hold together

ways of night. Noticing
the sound feel inside feet
that rhythm the old poems
winding like finding high.

In the Time Body Together

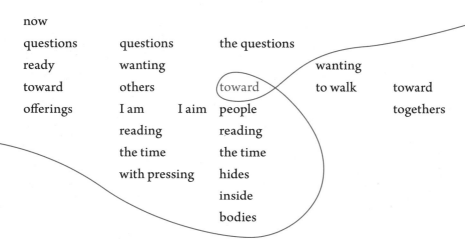

now
questions   questions   the questions
ready   wanting   wanting
toward   others   toward   to walk   toward
offerings   I am   I aim   people   togethers
               reading   reading
               the time   the time
               with pressing   hides
                                 inside
                                 bodies

how it breaks and toys really ways the reading into knowing the now
of my pleasing pace of languaging

I thinking time I
raid the feelings read
the body weigh the
wanting
questions autistic reading   questions

thinking yous and leaving   the time
toward readers together and

                                 question
                                 willows
                                 pleasing
                                 poetry

Eros of Bathing Stimming Dancing Pacing

Mostly I want to rake in the people
to understand the ways of pacing real thoughts
the feeling way

pace pace pace the talking
and type type type the thinking

and the two will rally
and become

Pace names the ways of thinking
and typing feels the ways of pacing

every string games
the perfect love in movement
in real relation
with inspirational rights
of people like me

Having the lust dancing in giving life to feel
the names of categories dancing
out of bounds
is amazing to play

and I get a thrill guessing
the way people will respond
to me and my open
languaging

language is the pavement answering
the way and I am the water
bathing and living
lustfully

Main idea in the eros of autism is the pace
dancing so I feel
fantastic like rallying ocean waves
carrying me like a boogie
board of puttering
on top of the warm water

Mind is lavishing
in the ideas in the eros
pacing
give me some examples

Love the power I have been bathing autistically
and living stimming dancing

the pacings
opening that field of thinking toward
artful liberation

from people who think autism is a problem
and janitors of diversity
live in that world

where simple cleanup
is bigger problem

lusting real ludicrous idea
that we need clean perfect people

I fastly make need
jumping always
on the page

Ways of Neurodivergent Time

Good language is
the way the walks think
about the time.

Making the ways of questions
is the ways
of thinking openly and
I want the ways
to be full
of them like answers
that find open
air to
take far
reaching ideas for
a right
to roll.

The line
pacing thinking is
never straight but falls
and goes in many
directions.

The language of the
time never opens to
the language of
the dance
that opens time.

Resting is the nonthinking
time, but for me
easy walking is
hard because
the falling I fall
into the dance
of real at mospheres that feel like
too much and using every buttress I can find will anchor me
and help me to calmly start walking
toward my destination.

The ways
I make
the walking
work dreams
of a world
where the
dance opens the
dreaming grieving ways
for the way neurotypical bodies can't dream varied ways of cities
are longing
for real game
of feeling.

Place of dreaming
is here are families outing the
making inward iterations
or are
they making lines in the
sand of time?

152

The ways
of families
are pacing all the
same, but the nattering neurotypicality is the always pressure
of not varying pace, but of bettering time
to be the same.

The Ripples Are Ongoing Acts

The moon
of the lake
is accurate.

Am I big
enough for
the pull?

Yes let's
write about
the pullings
of waters.

How small we
are to the water
would trigger
the ways.

Inviting the ways
of compassion
to each: offerings.

The ripples greatly
sew the stitches
of beings. Are we
good? Can we
be good?

How much water
does it take to
drown us, pull us
into awakenings?

I want us to pull
and pull into each
other's ripples and
pull out the smallness
of the human in us.

Notes

I loved writing these poems that language differently. About the weekly writing I want to say that the rallying engagement with others is important because it is a way of the buttressing relation that happens. I made this work by talking with others: Chris Martin, Ellen Bleiwas, and my mom, Estée Klar. They are in conversation with me about ideas and we think together about leaving forms that resist the neurodiverse makings that we need. I think that my languaging opens the meanings of "what is neurodiversity" and that is important to understand how I bathe in the atmospheres that call me to answer. Languaging the way I relate to the moving words—they are lasting and fleeting and pacing the bathing ecologies we are in, but neurotypicality wants to cut and cure my ways in terms of pathology, and opening phrases the way I do is like water-pathing and easy-thinking.

I am always reading and language is bathing me and giving me the varied dances of living. I am that person who could read from an infant age and I am not able to forget that. I now name things in streams of feeling making sentences that calm and free the open moving mind with the body making dances, not games. In the typing movement that I need to communicate in my life, I am answering and rallying a new way because I think in between the type. Words slow me down but this is part of my writing style.

Acknowledgments

"Answers Towards Questions Other Than What is Autism," "In Way of Music Water Answers," and "A Typology of Water," appeared in *Explicit Literary Journal*.

"Tall Ideas" appeared in the Academy of American Poetry's Poem-a-Day series.

Several of these poems have also been featured by the Disability Visibility Project's Access Is Love show.

Thank you to my collaborators, to my loving family, friends and assistants, and to Milkweed publishing.

Michael Klar

ADAM WOLFOND is a nonspeaking autistic artist, prose writer, and poet. He has two poetry chapbooks, *In Way of Music Water Answers Toward Questions Other Than What Is Autism* and *There Is Too Much Music in My Ears,* and is the co-founder of dis assembly, a neurodiverse arts collective in Toronto.

⅌ multiverse

Multiverse is a literary series devoted to different ways of languaging. It primarily emerges from the practices and creativity of neurodivergent, autistic, neuroqueer, mad, nonspeaking, and disabled cultures. The desire of Multiverse is to serially surface multiple universes of underheard language that might intersect, resonate, and aggregate toward liberatory futures. In other words, each book in the Multiverse series gestures toward a correspondence—human and more-than-human—that lovingly exceeds what is normal and normative in our society, questioning and augmenting what literary culture is, has been, and can be.

milkweed
EDITIONS

Founded as a nonprofit organization in 1980, Milkweed Editions is an
independent publisher. Our mission is to identify, nurture, and publish
transformative literature, and build an engaged community around it.

Milkweed Editions is based in Bdé Óta Othúŋwe (Minneapolis) within
Mní Sota Makhóčhe, the traditional homeland of the Dakhóta people.
Residing here since time immemorial, Dakhóta people still call Mní Sota
Makhóčhe home, with four federally recognized Dakhóta nations and many
more Dakhóta people residing in what is now the state of Minnesota. Due to
continued legacies of colonization, genocide, and forced removal, generations
of Dakhóta people remain disenfranchised from their traditional homeland.
Presently, Mní Sota Makhóčhe has become a refuge and home for many
Indigenous nations and peoples, including seven federally recognized Ojibwe
nations. We humbly encourage our readers to reflect upon the historical
legacies held in the lands they occupy.

milkweed.org

Milkweed Editions, an independent nonprofit publisher, gratefully acknowledges sustaining support from our Board of Directors; the Alan B. Slifka Foundation and its president, Riva Ariella Ritvo-Slifka; the Amazon Literary Partnership; the Ballard Spahr Foundation; *Copper Nickel*; the McKnight Foundation; the National Endowment for the Arts; the National Poetry Series; the Target Foundation; and other generous contributions from foundations, corporations, and individuals. Also, this activity is made possible by the voters of Minnesota through a Minnesota State Arts Board Operating Support grant, thanks to a legislative appropriation from the arts and cultural heritage fund. For a full listing of Milkweed Editions supporters, please visit milkweed.org.

Interior design by Tijqua Daiker and Mary Austin Speaker
Typeset in Arno

Arno was designed by Robert Slimbach. Slimbach named this typeface after the river that runs through Florence, Italy. Arno draws inspiration from a variety of typefaces created during the Italian Renaissance; its italics were inspired by the calligraphy and printing of Ludovico degli Arrighi.